I Can Pray to God

written by Sandra Brooks

illustrated by Lois Axeman

God gave me two hands.

He gave me a right hand
and a left hand.

Each hand has four fingers and a thumb.

My thumb closes over my fingers so that I can pick up things. Try to pick up something without using your thumb. Can you do it?

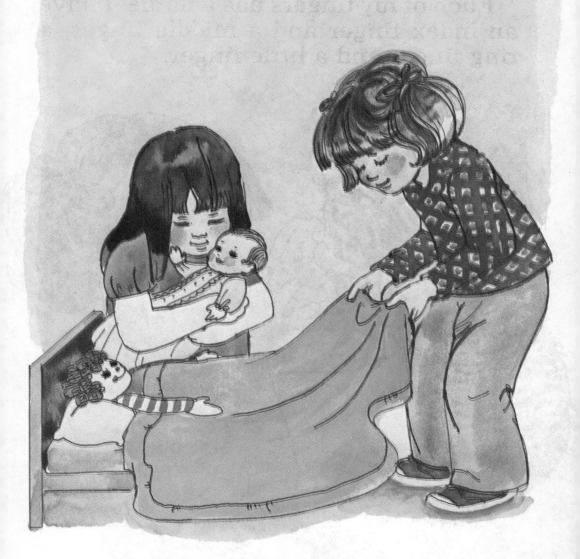

Each of my fingers has a name. I have an index finger and a middle finger, a ring finger and a little finger.

Sometimes people call the little finger the pinky.

I can use my hands to play.

I can use them for coloring in my coloring book,

for crossing the monkeybars at the playground,

and for bringing my Mommy a bouquet of flowers.

I can use my hands to work.

I can use them for helping Mommy set the table,

for picking up the toys in my room,

and for giving my dog some
food and water.

When I pray, I fold my hands together.

My hands help me to remember to pray for others.

Since my thumb is closest to my heart, it reminds me to pray for everyone I love most—like Mommy and Daddy and my relatives and friends.

Preachers and teachers sometimes point their index fingers when they teach a lesson. This reminds me to pray for preachers and teachers.

My middle finger stands high above all my other fingers. This reminds me to pray for our President and other people in government.

The ring finger is the weakest finger on my hand. It reminds me to pray for people who are sick and unhappy.

The last finger on my hand stands for me. By praying for myself last, I learn to think of what other people need as well as myself.

I learn to do as Jesus said. He said that I should love my neighbor as myself. My neighbor is anyone I know about. So I should love and pray for anyone I know about.

When I pray, I can thank God for my hands, and for people around me for whom I pray.